ALL THESE HUNGERS

ALL THESE HUNGERS

Rick Mulkey

BRICK ROAD
POETRY PRESS

Brick Road Poetry Press
www.brickroadpoetrypress.com

For Susan and Hunter

Library of Congress Control Number: 2021934338
ISBN: 9781950739035

Published by Brick Road Poetry Press
314 Lee Road 553
Phenix City, AL 36867
www.brickroadpoetrypress.com

Brick Road logo by Dwight New

Table of Contents

Concerning Whisky...3

I.
Cured...7
Mingo County Men...9
Gestation..10
Curse Poem..11
Refugee..14
Waking Alone After Drinking Too Much Wine in Umbria........15
Considering the Continued Use of Insects as Literary Metaphors.......16
What Remains..18
Why I Browse the Hardware Store...19
Gender Studies: How Men Fail at Small Talk.............................21
Pickling Crock...22
In Defense of Haggis..23

II.
Where are you, Walt Whitman?..29
Then the Journalist Asked How Did We Arrive Here.................31
America the Beautiful...33
Velveeta...34
Hurricane Season, Tampa...35
American Made...36

III.
An Explanation...41
Becoming..43
Waiting for Bread in My Grandmother's Kitchen.......................44
After Ruysch's *Still-Life with Fruit and Insects*............................45
Pinto Beans..46
Domestic Architecture..47
What You Have to Understand..48
Lemonade Pantoum...50
Threnody...51

IV.
The Language of Rivers..55
Gentle Butchery..57
False Spring..58
Freestone Peach..59
Cheerleaders at Forty..60
Explicating Bluefield...61
A Scatological Scat...62
Why I Miss the Circus...63
Workday..64

Tool Box...65
What They Drank...67

Notes..69
Acknowledgments..70
About the Author..72

I believe in the flesh and in the appetites
        —Walt Whitman, "Song of Myself"

There is communion of more than our bodies when bread is broken and wine drunk.
        —M.F.K. Fisher, *The Gastronomical Me*

The world begins at a kitchen table...Perhaps the world will end at the kitchen table,
        while we are laughing and crying, eating the last sweet bite.
        —Joy Harjo, "Perhaps the World Ends Here"

Concerning Whisky

Potent, peaty, brine-filled dram
like the salt-washed rocks of sheltered bays;
like the turf fires beneath thatched roofs; like rain
falling hard and soot blackening the stone hearth;
like the venerable who curl into themselves
and wait for spring, old women, grown diaphanous,
who flutter like moths embalmed in their silver-haired cocoons,
aged, at last, into their ghostlier selves; like their men
no longer storming pastures as fierce scouring winds,
but, lost in their suffering, now gnaw remorse
and grasp at guilt as they once did pipe and pint.

This is the alchemy of fire and air, the chemistry of creek and valley.
The distillate of place and time. Distillate of memory.
Soft, sugary, amber-clouded elixir like the lure
of meadowsweet and chicory, like October smoke
hanging over maple and oak; like the sophistry of sex
on sunlit mornings in late December,
cold hands along the flushed length of spine and breast,
breath passing across the altar of tongue, frosting bedroom windows;
like the dulcet notes of mandolin, the sorrowful soaring of fiddle;
the primal groan of Cash's *Ring of Fire*,
or Elvis's moaning call to *Love Me Tender*.

This is the push and pull, the liquid mystery train
of peril and possibility we can't explain
though it carries a little of everything: the bog, the raisin,
the raison d'etre, the pie safe and gun safe, the morning promises
and midnight faults, the scars forgotten and reclaimed,
the ice, in expectation, clanging in a glass.

I

Cured

for Albert Goldbarth

Albert, I'm here to tell you
Bluefield, Virginia has the best bacon
in the eastern U.S. I know
you've never been there, but it's the kind
of place you might visit on a Sunday,
clear blue sky and mountain ridges frosted,
when all the evangelicals in their aging
chapels and strip mall sanctuaries are off to pray
that folks like you and me won't turn
their fruitful lands into a salty waste,
and you'd be left alone
or nearly so, in the only diner
open on a Sunday morning. Just like me
you'd be lured in by the satisfying
aromas of peppered pork belly, the sensation
of eating the blistered fat of swine.
We wouldn't care that it was spiritually unclean,
or that all it touched was unclean,
the unclean plate, the unclean scrambled eggs,
the filthy toast and jam, the way our fingers
lathered in its fatty sweetness
were unclean, or our mouths unclean,
or the BLT we'd order to take
with us, piled high in bacon, unclean.
And later, as we walked the empty streets
before the local parishioners labored out
to find their way home to sanctified roasts
they'd ravage from pristine platters,
you and I and our friends would grow hungrier
and hungrier as we'd compare the subtle flavors
of acorn and truffle, the sugary-salty depth of pig.
Then you'd quote from Su Shi, Martial,

7

or Matthews' sensuous song of swine,
"Sooey Generous," and we'd agree that eventually
we'll all be offered up on one altar or another,
salted with fire and smoke, salted with age, salted
in baths, entering a covenant of salt, cured,
if you will, of any worries about what might
come to pass tomorrow. And knowing this life
is the one life and wanting to make the most of it,
we'd pick up a glass of very cold, very sweet tea
at the Dairy Queen, and we'd unwrap our sandwiches,
drink deeply from the cup, and eat of the crispy flesh,
satisfied celebrants of this porcine priesthood.

Mingo County Men

When I knew them as boys
shooting spit wads at Principal Martin
and sneaking peeks at the fishnet hose
of our young 4th grade teacher Ms. McCall,
they already sneered like grown men
with jobs as haul truck drivers
or longwall miners for Independence Coal.

They already had wives whose girlhood
dreams had fallen flat as cakes
dislodged from Easy Bake Ovens,
whose cheerleader smiles were swapped
for a Bud and a bottle of Oxy.

Even then, slipping on sneakers
instead of steel-toed boots, their houses had an air
of lumberyard sawdust and coal-tar pitch.
Their lunches carried the stench of onions
and potted meat. Their hands, stained yellow
by Camels they'd snatch from their father's packs,
were already calloused and gashed.

And how they dropped then crushed
the finished butts beneath their feet
said failure; though, they still stood,
that harness of smoke encircling them, watching
and waiting for their futures to begin.

Gestation

Above plowed rows, the sun turned hot and sour
while she tested the shade of maple leaves.
Pregnant and sweating from her morning's labor,
bushel basket of beans to snap and freeze,
she rocked the front porch glider.
Its song, phrased more with rust than metal,
suggested all days are brief and passing.
Flies hummed in fresh-turned compost and manure
which each spring constructed her garden.
Corn and squash she'd can and shelve, would soon
come on, then later she'd pickle crocks of beets.
Meanwhile, the child inside her wrenched and kicked,
and, years before they'd wake, cancer cells deep
inside her breasts cleaved to their fertile sleep.

Curse Poem

It would be easy at the end of a day
of demoralizing disappointments
and misanthropic misdemeanors, to let loose
with a series of fucks, motherfucks,
and goddamns. Science even suggests
it might make us feel better
if not force the world to make sense.
It's what my son assumed when he was seven
and with his mother when they nearly came,
as my high school coach, most vulgar man
I ever knew, used to say, as close
as a "cunt hair" to a head-on collision.
He turned to his mother, both breathless with fear
and said, "It makes me want to say something bad."
"Go ahead," she offered, which he did,
his first F-bomb exploding its syllabic shrapnel
across the dashboard. For a moment,
he did feel better. Though feeling better
is not what this poem is about. Or feeling worse
for that matter. This is a poem about language,
words to be specific, and how they can profess love
or rage, how they can enlighten or disguise,
endear or destroy. How a 15-year-old girl, alone
and living on the streets can be convinced
to perform acts she couldn't have imagined
by a pimp sharing a bubble-gum pink Icee,
and telling her, in the words she'd longed to hear
from her country-clubbing mother
and cheating father, "I understand you."
Maybe we all are cursed by our various lexicons,
cursed to describe and explain, cursed to extol,
cursed to pretend. Cursed as much
by the start-of-day "good morning"
as we are by the close-of-day "good night."

Cursed to believe we can comprehend any of it.
There are, of course, those who say words are incapable
of expressing meaning, or mean
something other than what we try to express.
Jeffrey Eugenides suggests we need
"Germanic train-car constructions" in place of single word emotions.
No room for joy, but rather "the happiness that attends disaster."
Maybe the long-married couple piled into their
king-sized bed, all that empty space around them, have it right.
She's watching the *Late Show with Stephen Colbert*
and he's reading *Anna Karenina* considering
how "there are no conditions to which a person
cannot grow accustomed." He's listening to her laugh
at jokes not nearly as funny as his own when he wonders
why they practice what not to say until they say nothing
effortlessly. And why not this silence,
given there never were enough words,
or the right words for love's many hungers.
Yet, it's words a son tries to find at his mother's death bed.
She's gone, at least her mind is, and she's lost
all words by now, can't say them, can't form them
on her dried lips, possibly can't even recognize them,
and still he's looking for the right ones. He knows
he'll remember these words even if she won't.
He knows he'll take them with him after
others have said more words in the church,
and more words by the grave, and late at night
months and even years later he'll wake to those
syllables, each vowel of pain, each consonant of guilt
forming a sentence that sours on the tongue.
And in that night he'll hear his mother's voice
as he did as a child when he'd cursed her for being his mother.
"I will make thy tongue cleave to the roof of thy mouth,
that thou shalt be dumb," a kind of curse she repeated

as she forced his head to the sink, lifted the soap,
and scoured every word from his mouth.

Refugee

We all know a little something of exile,
the way the sun abandons January,
the exodus of wrens from jasmine
in late August. For the Alzheimer's patient
the body is a foreign land and every face
a stranger's. My mother-in-law's
exile sighs along gated walls
and vanishes beyond the front door
like all the beaches she ever walked.
It picks the locks in her dreams at night,
steals each memory and texture,
then scatters them, salting the earth.

Waking Alone After Drinking Too Much Wine in Umbria

after Li Po

Jasmine rises on the backs of sun-soaked walls
while swifts and swallows perfect a calligraphy of wind and wing.

Not much of a hangover to speak of, there is little
to worry me, save an abandoned skirt

mocking from its laundry line.
The scent of coffee lingers in doorways

and alleys the sun works ceaselessly to fill.
Beside me on the balcony, the oleander

in its cracked pot grows too large, refuses
to be tamed, refuses to hide in shadow

when there is so much Mediterranean light.
When I notice its bloom is more the deep claret

of autumn than the crimson of August,
I imagine I hear flies in the tomato fields,

vines drying and fruit beginning to blacken,
rotting from bottom to stem.

And afraid to find one more life to grieve,
I grab my glass, pour another drink of wine large enough

to give reason to laugh with whatever joy
I have left, then wait for the evening

silhouette of swifts to startle my heart
into some other life.

Considering the Continued Use of Insects as Literary Metaphors

after Hayden Carruth

So many of them crushed beneath a boot,
captured and released from a grandmother's tissue,
slurped up in evening hatches by brown
and cutthroat trout. And so many poems
about them, and most of those concerning
love and grief, those two heart-sore twins
we seem unable to understand without
the metaphorical biting mandibles of hopper
and tick, the piercing sting of wasp:
Donne's flea, Keats's cricket, Dickinson's buzzing fly,
and Neruda's lust-filled generic crawler
making its way across a lover's hip, to name a few.
So many, in fact, it's hard to calculate
the reams of paper it has taken to print them all.
Still that number doesn't come close
to matching the population in this one
nest of fire ants bustling just beyond
my summer hammock. All of us,
meaning humans, don't add up
to the ant colonies populating one square mile
in any home town. Yet, without them,
the world would fall apart. That can't be
said for us. Let some pandemic virus
wipe us out and the world keeps going,
flourishing even. This is why,
towering above these ants
with my can of Raid, I consider what
a waste of effort this is, what a waste
of life, not just theirs but my own,
which, pandemic or not, is ending
faster than I'd like. And I find myself

giving way to grief and sorrow,
like so many others. This,
I say out loud to the insects,
is the finishing off of humankind.
They show no interest in my declarations,
ignoring me with the same lack of devotion
reserved for other ignored gods
before they disappeared into the booklice-
riddled pages of epic and myth. I don't know
if insects understand. I don't know if they wake
at night to name the constellations,
or grieve those drowned by flooding storms.
But I'm pretty sure they won't write poems
about me and my hammock afternoons,
nor consider my hands and mouth
as metaphors for colony collapse,
nor pause from all their constant work,
when the last man or woman passes
beyond the need for rhyme and simile,
to say goodbye.

What Remains

Here in the garden with arugula wilted,
blackberries finished, and snow peas not quite ready,

we're pulling weeds and suckering tomatoes.
Tossing blighted plants to one pile for burning, ripened

Romas, knotted and imperfect, to the other pile
for canning, I consider how so much of our marriage

followed this ritual, a paring down of clutter,
a culling and clarifying of what we needed

from each other. Pausing to wipe sweat from your cheek,
you check your reflection in the spade, catch me admiring.

Later, I'll write this moment down so it remains
no matter what we lose or fail to remember.

For now we work quietly in mild morning heat,
the winter we know will arrive still distant and restrained.

Why I Browse the Hardware Store

The wonder of the Home Depot is how common
all the wonders really are, nails and hammers,
wrenches of a dozen types, screws and pipes.
Each tool fashioned to a purpose, capable of assembly
and disassembly, of resolving any complication
with a simplicity of action we could easily
define as a form of beauty.
Walking the aisles this late winter morning,
considering unfinished work
the coming spring will want addressed,
I remember an earlier hardware store,
the lumberyard lovers parked behind,
the marvels of strawberry-scented hair
filling the Ford, how my high school girlfriend's camisole
rested so soft beneath my clumsy hands
for a moment I was confused as to what was
satin and what was flesh,
and how each day since, I've lived exposed
to love's ceremonies I rarely understand.

Though, honestly, that was a time before love,
before I'd heard any man or boy I knew
speak it, except maybe to describe
a game-winning tackle on a Friday night.
I'd heard fathers gathered around a picnic table
discuss a porterhouse in ways that elevated it
to a state of loveliness, and their sons
did the same beneath a Camaro's polished hood,
holding pliers and spark plug wrenches
in their grease-caked hands.
That was before I'd discovered Coltrane or Ravel,
before John Donne rested on my nightstand.
I knew nothing of the longing of Botticelli,
or the beauty of women in their morning robes

sipping coffee and buttering toast.
But I'd seen and heard women alone
listening to Patsy Cline on the turntable
sing *I Fall to Pieces*.

I'd seen them cry, body-shaking,
chest-gasping sobs that splintered a life
into more fragments than vice or nail
could hold together.
And I'd wanted to reach for them, tell them it,
whatever it was, would be okay.
I'd wanted to say the word love
in the hope that it would open into them
like a stent, fill all those fractures.
But that was never what was needed.
The heart in its tenuous frame
can't shape love square and plumb.

Which is why I'm browsing the garden center
for mulch and fertilizer, for pruning shears and spade
my wife will want. She hasn't given up
on the jasmine and lilies in our hard clay soil,
the ones that somehow overcame both
the summer-long drought we thought
would burn it all, and the late-winter floods
we believed nothing could survive,
especially those delicate petals, light
as a camisole cast off by lovers' hands.

Gender Studies: How Men Fail at Small Talk

"The Southern Right Whale has a penis 10 feet long," she tells him. He's not sure whether he should be impressed or embarrassed. On another occasion, she points out that the male dragonfly, after mating, severs its body from its prick leaving it in the female. "O.K.," he offers, "I've read around. I know about those castrating female characters of the 1920's novels. I'm a product of the Carter years. I understand some men have become pacifists, that Camille Paglia wants us on occasion to act like we really do have balls. But what are you getting at?" "Nothing," she says. "Just thought you'd like to know." "Listen," he says. "I watch football some Saturdays, especially the SEC, and I've been to a hockey game or two, and when I was younger I could put away cheap beer, you know the kind you'd use coupons for at Krogers, with the very best of them. And hell, I used to hunt. Never killed anything, but I might have. So, just because I know what cheese goes with what wine, and just because I've got this thing for Martha Stewart, especially when she's up to her elbows in compost, and just because I make the best damn scones this side of Ireland, don't think I'm not as much man as any whale or dragonfly." "I thought you'd be interested," she says, her voice already distant, her face already turned away. "Well, I'm not," he says. "I'm not."

21

Pickling Crock

My god the smell could waste you.
Even the flies turned up their noses
and flew off to barns and pasture.

Our brine-stung lungs would fester
breathing the vinegary rot. We'd open windows,
still, my god, the smell would waste you.

So each cabbage and cuke could sour into rapture,
the women understood more than others,
their men and children off in barns and pasture,

the importance of salt and patience to avoid disaster:
pickles slick and soft as minnows
with a taste and smell that could waste you.

Today, unsealing a jar after trying to master
my mother's recipe, I think how memory opens
on the tongue and nose, images of barns and pastures,

where close but not exact results in disappointing gestures.
So don't compare, I think. Enjoy what chance exposes:
the pleasure of kraut so pungent it could waste you
for anything sweet, memory of pickles savored by barn or pasture.

In Defense of Haggis

The name doesn't help, "hag"
right from the start unsettling
the leery diner who, already filled
with culinary horror stories
of organs, blood and intestinal
sheaths, is certain a hag is
not what you want to wrap
your mouth around.
And I get it. I, too, have watched
in wretched disgust at the sight
of other "delicacies" ravished,
the pickled pigs feet
my mother and father ate,
sucking the hoof and bone,
slurping the gelatinous cream
of pork fat and marrow,
delving tongue-deep into the intimate
innards of swine. And that's how it was
before gluten-free crackers and tofu,
when you raised what you ate,
cared for it, even let your daughter
name it, then come November
and the frost, and the ground
grown solid, you'd rise early,
lead the animal, no name
required on that day,
to the slaughter shed,
kill it and watch the last quake
in the thigh, the graying over
of the eye; then you'd skin and clean it,
parse it into all the refined parts:
the loin, the chop, the roast, the ham,
then the shanks and rib, until all
that was left was the offal,

23

the cast-offs, the leftover, the undesirable.
These are the good bits,
the naughty bits, food of the poor,
of the serf, the slave, the peasant,
the tenant and migrant, the miner.
Every culture has a version:
goetta, pannas, sujuk, krakowska,
black pudding, white pudding, groaty pudding,
livermush, boudin, and scrapple.
And why not celebrate the remainders,
the vestigial, the wonder of finding
Sunday's half-eaten pot roast turned
to Monday's toast with creamed chip beef,
the Wednesday morning breakfast fashioned
from Tuesday night's cashew chicken;
or the college girlfriend I never loved
but tried to, hoping not to hurt her,
and the fish heads she'd feed the neighbor's cat,
and the stories she'd tell from the scraps
of her life, those residual pains and horrors
that kept us together beyond
our expiration date. Later, months after she'd left
and I'd moved on to other cities, other
names I'd learned to whisper, it became
the letters she'd written and never sent,
the ones her mother mailed to me after
they'd found her daughter's body in the bath,
an accident, a fall and blow to the head.
Suddenly leftovers were everywhere,
as common as estate sale knick-knacks,
the empty pants legs draped from the knees
of the double amputee I'd pass each morning.
They were the wine-stained
lire discovered in a pocket of a backpack
from the summer trip with that same woman.

They were youth hostel and B&B receipts, photographs
stuffed into a shoe box, sepia-saturated
along their Kodak-framed edges.
They were the borders of maps
and countries; borders along bodies
I once knew as well as my own.
So here I am thinking of the bits and pieces
of a life, thinking of haggis,
and how the liver and suet, the oats,
and especially the heart, tossed together
form something greater than themselves,
how the steam rises from the silver tray it's carried on,
how the earthiness of cracked pepper and nutmeg,
the aromatic thyme fill the room,
and I like to think our lives have space
for the dignity found in the struggles
of the unnoticed and unappreciated,
of those young mothers and fathers feasting
on whatever marrow life brings them,
so when the first forkful is lifted
our lips purse into a joyous "O" of surprise.

II

Where are you, Walt Whitman?

In all people I see myself, none more and not one a barley-corn less,
And the good or bad I say of myself I say of them.
 —Walt Whitman, "Song of Myself"

Where are you, Walt?
The Open Road goes to the used-car lot.
Where is the nation you promised?
 —Louis Simpson, "Walt Whitman at Bear Mountain"

Where are you, Walt Whitman? With the inaugural guests who showed
    up early
wearing buttons and waving flags while a white man
in a MAGA hat recites an allegiance? Or are you holding a protest sign,
chased by police down alleys, or corralled in holding areas
in parks where blades of grass are trampled down?
Surely you didn't arrive in a limo wearing a Hermes tie
and Gucci loafers, editing a list of all the ills your kind has suffered.
Please tell me that wasn't you. Maybe, Walt Whitman,
you refused to attend. Paid no attention to the TV crews or barricades;
instead, walked six miles to work in a hotel laundry, cleaned pots in an
    all-night diner.
Was that you hunched over in a bean field? Or cutting your palms
on corn husks? Or driving tuxedo-clad senators in your checkered cab?
Walt Whitman, I was awake election night crying while a woman
in Kentucky sang praises that her god was stronger
than me and mine. What song did you sing, Walt Whitman?

If you are all of us, you, too, must have cried, but also cheered,
and you must have gloated and mourned, shouted in joy,
dropped your head in disbelief. Did you really believe
everyone's invited to the party? Including this woman on CNN
who likes "alternative facts," or this man in the grocery line
who doesn't know what to believe since the tabloids
offer no clues? Or this one who only wants her deported sister back,
or the one in the airport cuffed and hauled away?
How can you stand to be them all, Walt Whitman?

How can you stand to be you? How can you still sing your song?

Oh, Walt, where are you now? Where are you hiding?
Are you the one bleeding in an Afghani barrack?
Are you the one nestled in the fast food wrappers inside the trash
    dumpster?
Perhaps that's you watching the gathering crowd from your K Street
    office window.
Maybe you are the one that lost a job, lost a child, lost yourself
inside the towering bills and notices. Maybe you are
the high school student cowering in a closet, listening for the AR 15's
crack and thump, the journalist struggling for facts,
the poet afraid words no longer mean as they once did
when you resounded over lines as far reaching as empire itself.
Now we find America's epic compressed to a singularity, weighted
    down
by 240 characters, where the elected shaman is a used car salesman
twittering his song from a king-sized bed, an aria claiming all of this
and all of us are "Lies, Lies, Lies. Sad. Sad. Sad."
Once, Walt Whitman, *we were together. I forget the rest.*

Then the Journalist Asked How Did We Arrive Here

First someone killed someone else.
First someone pointed a Glock,
or accelerated an engine, or thrust a knife.
First someone yelled "Fuck you" and shook
their banner at someone else.
First someone threw a brick
through a synagogue window and watched
as glass shattered into irreparable pieces.
First a group marched hoping to stop
the group that carried torches.
First a group showed up carrying torches,
tiki lamps from American owned mega-chain
department stores or home and garden shops.
First thousands of men, and even some women,
confused freedom with capitalism, confused
opportunity with disenfranchisement,
confused equality with domination.
First someone's hate was given voice and power.
First a demagogue inflamed hate
and division to enhance his own power.
First someone felt hate without remorse.
First someone was taught to hate.
First a child played and knew only
what the world showed him.
First a newborn child breathed and cried
because this world seemed strange
and cold and all the child had known
was warmth, the sound
of a woman's voice and a man's voice
somewhere beyond what he could see.
First a child was conceived.
First two people met and fell in love,

and they were absolutely certain
their world was better for it.

America the Beautiful

On any given day in America,
in any marbled capital city, cineplex-
filled suburb or oak-lined main-street
nestled beyond fields of corn and wheat,
pine-skirted mountains casting shadows
over prairies cross-hatched with highways,
somebody you know, or used to know,
or never met but looked familiar
or not familiar at all, will stick a Glock
to someone's brow, pull the trigger
then drive away. A moment later,

the wind will carry
the odor of gunpowder down the street
where a boy mowing the lawn
will catch the scent and think of BBQ,
how hungry he is and how later
he'll have a hot dog with relish
at the minor league game that night
and maybe even a Coke, while beside him
his kid sister will stuff the end
of a Mars bar in her mouth then stand
and sing full-throated with all the spectators,

"America! America!"

Velveeta

As a child, I thought of you as cheese,
something like a cheddar or muenster,
or even camembert, all those options we never
invited into our house. Served on refried beans,

or on a plate with crackers, melted in bowls
for dipping, or between grilled toast.
Broccoli grew up with you, as did casseroles
and tacos. There would have been no burger

and fries without you melted over
at least one. No Thanksgiving without you
in the mac and cheese. No sugar
hangover without you sliced tissue-

thin over apple pie. You're the most American
of all the cheeses; although, your inventor
was an immigrant farmer's son from Switzerland,
and you're not really cheese. You're a charter member

in the cheese product club, a pretender, a fake,
which is why you're so popular in our nation.
You rate high in favorability polls. You make
promises you only partly keep. If you were a politician

you'd be an orange-hued success, until,
as is often the case, enough people tasted
Manchego or Gorgonzola and finally distilled
how much time on your processed luxury they'd wasted.

Hurricane Season, Tampa

September, clusters of summer
leaves and seed pods tossed in the crest
of the storm gather like migrants
on the edges of lawn, street, and fence.
Rainwater backs up at the sewer grate,
holds a grudge, elbows out Styrofoam cups
and cigarette butts. Around the corner
the strip mall with its Mexican grocery
and small engine repair shop
stands mostly empty, boarded windows
and tattered palm fronds. A young woman,
toddler in tow and plastic grocery tote
slung over her shoulder, bends against
a downpour, act more of strength than attrition.
Her brown skin and eyes partially hidden
beneath her hood glisten with rainwater.
When I pull beside her to offer a ride,
her look of doubt and fear is as primal
as this wind. And like it, she will not slow down.
She will not be stopped.

American Made

I know someday you'll have a beautiful life
—Eddie Vedder

Tommy's mother never woke
in time to drive him to school,
never showed up to help
as 3rd grade homeroom parent,
or cheer for basketball games in Jr. High.
We never saw Tommy's mother chaperone
a Sadie Hawkins' Dance. And Tommy
rarely spoke of her or his father,
a disappearing act from years before
he imagined them both vanished
into the ether of a blackened box.
Though some nights during high school,

drinking Miller ponies, cruising the streets
of our small Virginia town, convertible tops down,
dreaming of women and sex, sports and sex,
7-Eleven burritos and sex, we'd come
across Tommy's mother turning tricks
by the railyard tracks on Princeton Ave,
twenty-dollar handjobs, thirty for her
mouth, or so we heard our fathers
chuckle while sipping Jack and Coke,
huddled around their charcoal grills,
manicured lawns smooth as billiard felt.

As 16-year-old boys, we laughed, too.
Laughed about the used condoms we left
in Tommy's school locker, laughed about
our own back-seat fumbling hands
and the salty taste of the body's hidden flesh,
laughed at the broken noses and busted lips
of parking lot brawls, laughed as we exposed ourselves

to any violent pleasure our lives could grasp.
But not Tommy bagging groceries at the IGA,
smoking at midnight by the Waffle House.
Festering in the back of chemistry class
like a teenage boy's boil, he simmered, flask
above a bunsen's flame, waiting in those moments
between volatile liquid and venting steam,
between the rib-caged violence of a heartbeat,
to pop just like an assassin's gun.

III

An Explanation

I know nothing of the way
a comet sings its melancholy song to the ether,
or how it scores its cold path repeatedly.

The sun and moon are as alien to me
as the colony of ants busily foraging, or the herd
of buffalo swaying in the prairie's tall grass.

I've little understanding of farm subsidies
or urban blight, of how a town called Prosperity
is little more than an abandoned Rite Aid store

boarded and smothered in kudzu,
all of it ditch weed scented, a breath the wind
trapped and forgot to exhale.

I know nothing of Wall Street bandits
or political priests in their great marbled halls.
There is little I can say about the rich

or the poor or women and children.
Or men either. And while I'm told
there are many gods and many prophets:

Jaweh, HaShem, Buddha, Vishnu, Shiva, Brighid,
Allah, and Muhammad, I fear there is
no god, no prophet, no shaman,

only profiteers and con men.
While there may exist an afterlife,
the cradling void is all we've discovered.

And though I want to understand
the intricacies of time, light, and the everlasting now,
how in the quantum world the future shapes the past,

these, and more, elude me. Instead, I sweep coal dust
from the floors of my mother's house
because I know that's what she'd do if still alive.

And she did it because it needed doing,
simple as that, a moment of grace.
How else to understand the comfort

this repetition offers, how else to explain
the rhythm of blood navigating veins,
wind surfing corn stalks, planets orbiting,

galaxies expanding. The raspy whisper
of broom straw across linoleum
calls me to the only prayer I know.

Becoming

Daily practice is what's called for,
like the ritual of morning prayer and evening prayer,
like the toddler's grasping hand on stair rails,
like the sincere *good morning* over breakfast toast.
Love the family more. Take time
to greet the neighbors. Be patient
in the Starbuck's line, tip the barista generously.
Always that desire to understand how to live
with that life we carry inside us.
As a boy I offered to clean
my piano teacher's attic because she was kind
and because she limped slightly from polio,
and because offering was what good kids did.
I swept and stacked, boxed and bagged.
Rearranged it all to make more sense.
Dusting a shelf, a box fell. Inside a fire agate ring
lost to a time no one in the house remembered.
I pocketed it in my jeans, aware of its weight,
its cold, gilded solidity, its spherical precision.
Downstairs my teacher offered tea and lemon,
thanked me with Chopin played on her Wurlitzer.
That was more than forty years ago
and what I've learned since is the man I'm becoming,
the one who understands little about perfection,
and only vaguely that feral hunger encircling us,
wants to return the ring to the box on its shelf,
but the boy, always believing in more,
keeps shoving his hand forever
deeper into his pocket.

Waiting for Bread in My Grandmother's Kitchen

This was before knotted hands could only watch
the dough kneaded, before age and labor
bent the back, before heartache bubbled up like yeast
in the chest and bloomed from the lips in an "O" of pain,
before emptiness in the stomach meant grief or cancer,
before worry had a definition or shape and so we worried
about dough's glossy sheen or lack of it,
whether anyone remembered to grease the pan,
what jelly or jam remained from last year's batch,
whether apples were falling uncollected on the ground;

and certainly before we fretted about carbs or gluten,
before we woke anxiously to news
streaming to us from electronic home assistants,
before friends and family lived as avatars in newsfeeds,
before we knew what the future could be since all we knew
of it was a wind-up timer on the kitchen counter,
the low wattage glow from the Kenmore oven;
this was the moment sourdough sweetened the air
while butter softened on the table, and in our mouths,
in that feral happiness of our mouths, we could already taste
the sacred ache and longing life never fully satiates:
ecstasy of bread melting on the tongue.

After Ruysch's *Still-Life with Fruit and Insects*

When sunset reaches through the open window
then crosses the canvas striking peaches into fire,
igniting grapes like oil lamps, highlighting melons
and plums arranged on the sideboard as if for supper,
it's tempting to think harvest and abundance,

but what of those eggs rotting in the nest,
the lizard scavenging shells, the beetle's
serrated jaw, the withered grape stem
and cracked chestnut, corn wasting in its husk,
wheat winnowing down to chaff?

How quickly the world comes to terms with endings,
flies already swarming the table scraps.

Pinto Beans

I shrank back from those brown-eyed
pods staring up from the bowl
my mother placed before me.

Ladled from the stove's cast iron pot,
steaming concoction signifying
another week of tightening belts
and dwindling possibilities.

Buttermilk cornpone, time card
of the underemployed, clocked in
by the soup spoon.

All afternoon my mother simmered
those small stones into submission,
seasoning with fatback and ground pepper.
We ate our fill, then asked for more.

Domestic Architecture

Closets are not the sort of thing most of us like to face.
—from a Realtor's web page.

We call them closets, but, in fact, they are
dioramas where we cast
pieces of ourselves. During storms,
occupations, relationships we can't escape,
they may act as shelters. Though, mostly,
they go unnoticed. When other rooms—
family room, dining room, bedroom—won't do,
too busy, too bright, too fraught with possibility,

we fill these fusty, vacant spaces
with all we fear revealed. Behind their doors,
a cache of what home hoped to be, what it was:
a tattered overcoat, empty anniversary vase,
discarded pocket knife. That peep-toe pump
with broken heel tossed into the corner.

What You Have to Understand

for my son

There's always more than is possible
to know: the inner workings
of a combustible engine;
the Christmas Eve assembly instructions
for a 16" Schwinn Cosmo; how a cat's paw
is both the padded tuft that stirs
you awake at night and the metal claw
which removes the nail binding
the house together; how *War and Peace*
takes up less digital space
than a typical Madonna pop video;
the reasons why our waistlines,
unlike Madonna's, keep
expanding after age 35; how to grow old
without growing old; how to manage
3:00 a.m. when sleep is the abandoned
husks of parasites descending
in moonlit dust; why we can't turn
a frittata into an egg, uncrumble a cookie,
unchisel the Pieta into a block of marble;
why it's always the past, the past, the past,
but we can never remember the future;
and why in the past we always had space
but now there is never enough;
how we build homes with more rooms
than we need, how we plan
with architects and designers the ways
to use each one or else some remain
as empty as a dementia-hollowed mind;
how it is when we see something marvelous,
say the miracle of Ruby Graupero-Cassimiro
dead 45 minutes before spontaneously resurrected,

we always ask *Is this live? Is this real?*
but never doubt the mundane;
and the moment you think you've learned it all,
contained each experience behind polished glass,
disinfected it in museum-filtered light, you realize
there are still so many trips to unpack, so many photos
of Renaissance fountains left to paste in albums,
so many wounds, reddened and scabbed, with stories
to re-enact, so many songs to write and play,
so much to relish that when you arrive
at the end of your life, you finally discover
what is meant by a true beginning.

Lemonade Pantoum

The worst are those mornings I wake believing
I've died and risen in Bluefield, Virginia,
resurrected on the crossroads of Route 460, somewhere
between what might lead to heaven or might not.

If you've died and risen in Bluefield, Virginia,
small towns with August lemonade might mean salvation,
might mean heaven to you, or might not. If you aren't careful,
you'll end up somewhere you're afraid to imagine. A place

where small towns and free August lemonade might save us
from worrying our existence, or believing the best days are ahead.
No, don't end up somewhere you're afraid to imagine, a place
where the Dollar General, boarded and empty, leans into kudzu.

I want to believe the best days are ahead, to exist
in a landscape worthy of praise, the valley where a lover's spine
leans into my hips, our storehouses empty and waiting, bodies like
    kudzu
coiled together, her sweet musk like berries in an Allegheny autumn.

The valley of a lover's spine, a geography worth mapping and praising.
The old Euclidean proofs won't help us understand these knots
coiled together, sweet berry musk of bodies in an Allegheny autumn.
I don't expect to rise eternally next to the woman I love. Though love,

salvation resurrected at the crossroads of two knotted bodies, is proof,
at least to me, of the need to sing of the sugared glaze of lovers
drinking lemonade and eating berries in places as dead-end lonely
and beautiful as Bluefield, Virginia.

Threnody

Mornings when their faces overwhelm me,
gathering like scratching hens by doorways,
I question how dead we can make the dead.
I fold, then box, abandoned skirts and ties.

I mark their graves with foxglove, then gather
with them on porch steps, play one final hymn,
hear rhythms resurrected in bloodroot
and laundry line, ballads only winds strum.

Always that audience refuses to leave,
even when the mandolin fades. The dead
enjoy the music for the sake of joy.
Only the living desire its sadness.

IV

The Language of Rivers

In the beginning, the language of rivers formed
beneath the stars when the earth first heard
the groaning lamentations of ice.

The language of rivers was ancient
before the first minnow grew the first gill
and darted without fear beneath the first eagle's shadow.

The language of rivers is the language of music:
the cacophony of canyons, the murmuration of dams
salmon migrate, the staccato notes of the deep plunge.

The language of rivers leaps
from the tongues of stones, stuns the sky
into silence, and outshouts the wind and storm.

The language of rivers is a deep gash
across the valley's naked spine,
black-winged like the conniving crow.

The language of rivers gives voice to basalt
tabernacles, choirs of riffles,
cut banks, flood plains and black pools.

The language of rivers possesses a dozen words
for sunlight: trout-shine, aurora salmonidae,
shoal-spawner, water-dancer.

The language of rivers has no word
for disease, or death, or man, but uses a dozen
words for life, all with feminine endings.

In the language of rivers, dawn
is not a noun for the start of morning,
but a verb for the final coital gasp.

In the language of rivers the name
for winter's full moon is the same word
used to describe the longing of north-flowing rivers.

In the language of rivers it is impossible
to be silenced by ruin. Even absence
holds matter, piles up like deadfall branches.

The language of rivers dams all feeling
until it breaks across a meadow where blackberry brambles
filled with finches shudder into being.

The language of rivers is a cracked chest
opening the heart to sleet and rain,
to thorns and unplowed earth.

The language of rivers descends
into the kingdom of roots and black loam.
It finds the world is anything but barren.

The language of rivers
remembers joy and sorrow have always lived here,
layered in the secret runnels of the body.

Gentle Butchery

Kneeling by Wolf Creek gutting the day's catch,
breath flew out of me,

all light pinched down to fish offal tossed
into the quickening current. What hold had I on life

or death? My dull blade and the trout's
open belly spoke for me,

for that wound no stitch could close.
Watching pines above the laurel pause their sway

as my lungs seized up and heart
refused, momentarily, its expected beat,

was a strange thrill, the way love's first touch
awakens us to a world where all we once knew

can't survive. And when my breath returned
from its downstream wanderings, and the white pines

once again rubbed their boughs
against the winter sky, I knew a part of me

had been carved away, leaving what remained more alive
and more mortal than when I'd stepped into the stream.

With each back cast, I breathed in as the hook soared past;
I breathed out with the hopeful looping fly.

False Spring

Charmed by the cherry's burlesque blossoms,
cafes open their doors
and fill the sidewalks with young women
in sleeveless dresses who tease
out each dusty ray of sunlight. Boys, hopeful,
as boys always are, laugh and strut
in that feral way that makes us
think of cranes in heat. And bees,
fascinated by false fruits, wander
the crystal rims of Chablis glasses.

Belief is everywhere, on the wind
shaking loose the last of autumn's
clinging leaves, on the backs
of tom cats stretching and yawning
into sun-pooled naps, in the way
the silence that grew all winter
beneath grey skies and frosted spruce
is duped into surrendering
to the garden-chatter of widows
who can barely catch their breath
so excited by the memory of spring
they've held tight to their chest.

They lower their faces to the earth,
inhale the soil, a scent like dusty clocks
and antique lace. Hands veined
into blue nests of promise and defeat,
they search the idle beds
for sprouting shoots or crocus buds,
for any sign of life that might stay
another bitter night, a return
to silence, and then to sleep.

Freestone Peach

How easily happiness begins
by eating it, this immortal fruit
of Queen Wang Mu, Tetons de Venus,
bivalved tree scallop, seed of the sun,
ambrosia of China Pearl, Summer Lady,
Garnet Beauty, Loring, Winblo,
Early Belle, and amulet of Alexander.
I split and plunder it, juice dripping
down my mouth and chin,
spilling peach flesh across my flesh,
fiber and sinew unhinged from the poisonous pit.
I lick and suck the seed; I ravish it down to stem.
Unburdened by the testament of bees
buzzing my beard, by the summer-scented stamen
of my thumb, by my stone-scraped tongue, by stains
upon my hands and lips, by the quickening loss
when I've finished the last one of the season,
I toss the few remains—peach-fuzz skin and sharp-
edged pit onto the compost pile to turn and steam.

Cheerleaders at Forty

They're in love again
with the old language of lunge and kick.
While others rush to work,
they're framed in windows at the local gym
training in Pilates, their children preened
and packed off to school, their husbands, former quarterbacks
and point guards, huddled in insurance office cubicles.
Even now their school girl voices overheard
in grocery stores and shopping malls
could rile the marching band's tight-lipped clarinetists
who hated them, their rouged cheeks,
mascara-lined eyes, their moussed hair,
how each sweater hid little from the crowd,
how they'd bend on hands and knees then rise in pyramids.
Despite the talk, few boys ever loved them
in breath-fogged Fords, desiring them most
haloed by stadium light in late September
before adolescence burned to cinders in factory fires.
Now at the gym they're pedaling stationary bikes,
swimming laps and hovering above ellipticals,
attempts to stop their universe from flying into entropy,
anything to halt the memory of their breath ghosting
in the cold of those Friday nights when the final whistle blew,
and the frost, without warning, began blooming all around them.

Explicating Bluefield

If you sound the body's deepest riddles,
map its secret paths from eyelash to thigh,
and leave with a longing that can only be
described as Bluefield, Virginia in April
when the air still tingles with the memory
of December and the hemlocks
stand frosted and silent at sunrise,
then flesh is no longer the jailer
that confines you, for ecstasy
reveals itself in all the hidden remnants
and moments, in ditchwater reflections,
in the unrelenting crow combing the alleys
and parks for the brilliance bound
in bottle caps and chewing gum foil,
in all the light might hold.

A Scatological Scat

Oh, what lovely fecal matter...!
   —Francois Rabelais

I who was a house full of bowel movement,
I who was a defaced altar
        —Anne Sexton

There's the shoo-bop-da-doo kind your mother doesn't mention
in front of company, and the kind your father jokes about.
There's the kind Victorians tried to hide, then industrialized.
With thanks to porcelain there's the mundane, routine,
some might even say pristine: the French rinsed
with their bidets, and the British loo built like piles
of books, all English titles. There's the kind beetles roll
into balls across savannahs. There are elephant mounds
large as haystacks, rhino patties washed and dried on racks,
then made into postcards for Kenyan tourist traps.
We have coprolites, gut casts, and the spiral groove.
Then there's the couple at the faculty party,
enough gin and tonic to petrify the heart.
For her the last three years passed in geologic time,
each real and imagined hurt gestating and calcifying
into a clenched fist: "You shit. You worthless little shit."
And he, with that smile she used to love,
nods as if to say, Yep, that's pretty much it.

Why I Miss the Circus

The circus comes as close to being the world in microcosm as anything I know.
—E.B. White

Because this teenage boy, slim-waisted and pants
hanging down, shuffles past Hammond's saw-mill
with its stacks of newly-cut pine boards;

because all day he proselytizes the merits
of wasted hours, the guilty pleasures of uselessness,
that rubber band propeller in his chest fallen slack and still;

because the lumberyard, meanwhile, hammers and saws,
singing the workday full with its ersatz hymn;
because corporate gods know we're easy to tame to the bridle;

because I'm old enough now to be happy praising this
boy cantering through the afternoon's bright sun,
wandering the midway to the center ring where clowns

crash their buggies into walls of exploding confetti,
where Spanish web-girls hang themselves
from aerial silks, and even the roustabouts

and riggers huffing one last smoke
tip-toe a high wire across a self-made heaven
too vast for any net to catch.

Workday

Roofers, even in the afterlife, can't stop
hauling the heft of asphalt shingles
on their humped shoulders, wincing at the bite
of the ladder's rung on each flattened arch.
Even now, in heaven or whatever this place
calls itself, the hammer and nail beat
the rhythm of a workday, sweat soaking
the Miller High Life t-shirt, eyes reddened
from the body's salt. And when the lunch break
arrives and the shade beneath the poplar and oak

withers to a thumbnail sliver, and the smell
of potted meat on white bread unwraps itself
from wax paper, the men turn to talk of beer
at the Moose Club or VFW, or the scent
of their wives in bed at night, the taste
and touch of skin along the ribs and hip,
and how the chance at rest is merely hours away,
a few more loads carried, another box of nails,
that quiet drive home past the cemetery,
the green grass resting beneath sun-bleached stones.

Tool Box

When he gave me the one his father had
given him, he said, "A good tool invites you
to pick it up." His were hands that held many.
Knew the difference between the weight
and balance of a ratcheting wrench
and a spark plug wrench. His were arms
that lugged power tools, hand tools,
vintage woodworking tools, garden tools,
and a lunch pail of the kind
no one owns anymore. His was
a back bent beneath the labor only men
and women used as tools can know.
Bent in the bean fields and hay fields,
bent by shingles carried up the roofer's
ladder, bent by the concrete mixer,
bent by the sledgehammer and shovel,
the jackhammer, the hoe and spade,
the engine block. His were palms
that knew other palms by their callouses
or lack of callouses. Knew my hands
were hands familiar with keyboards
and ballpoint pens, and understood
those were tools, too. Knew we all
were tools of war and power, tools of lust
and loss, tools that eventually lost
their use, grown weak from age,
rusted from neglect. When he asked me
to help with repairs after a storm,
I knew this was work he could no longer
do alone. I brought the toolbox with me.
I handed him a hammer and waited
to follow his lead as I always had,
knowing sometimes trying is all
that's asked. Sharing the small losses

this tinkering with our hands can almost fix.

What They Drank

Beer, the first beer, the one your uncle claimed would make you a man,
a Stroh's your tongue remembers swallowing, taste of a '70s tube sock;
Beer, the one turned sour beneath the backseat of your high school
  girlfriend's Scirocco;
Beer, the one left as a beached whale on the basin of the bathroom
  sink;
German Kolsch, English ale, Russian Imperial, India Pale;
Barrels of beer, mugs and steins of beer, beer in a $5 pitcher, beer in a
  bucket of ice;
Beer in your first English pub, Scottish pub, Irish pub,
Pilsner you turned down in Italy for a glass of Brunello;
Kronenbourg on the train before stepping into the stench of beer piss
  in the Gare du Nord;
Beer in the café, beer under the winter sky overlooking the
  Luxembourg Garden,
on the breath of the Danish woman you met there;
The traditional consummation bride-ale made for the bride and groom,
or the Babylonian honey beer made for the couple's lunar month
  "honey moon";
Beer residue in ancient Persian pottery jars, on clay tablets containing
  Sumerian poems,
in unearthed Mesopotamian pantries and cellars, in 7th-century
  monasteries;
Beer brewed first in homes by women, until men, as in most things,
  took it for profit;
The Stella the NY broker quaffs at The Full Shilling, celebrating
  success in the Bear market;
The fraternity beer keg the politician swaggers over in a college photo,
already certain of his future, his righteousness, his fluency in the
  dialogue of the deaf;
Beer stains on suit coats of grandfathers and fathers, the ones they
  wore to the grave.
Then there's the simple lager fetched from the kitchen fridge and
  poured in two mugs,

one each for the graying pair who lean over their steaming soup.
She lifts the spoon first to his lips, then to hers, asking if he remembers
the first meal they shared, for remembering is all she has now, and the
    one
thing he wants most. "Here," she says lifting the mug, "Take a sip.
You'll like it. It will make you feel better."

Notes

"Where are you, Walt Whitman?" concludes with a commonly misquoted passage of Whitman's from "Once I Pass'd Through a Populous City." The actual quote reads:

Day by day and night by night we were together—all else has long been forgotten by me

Acknowledgments

Thanks to the editors of the following publications where several of these poems appeared, some in slightly different form.

Appalachian Heritage: "Explicating Bluefield"
Baltimore Review: "Mingo County Men"
Crab Orchard Review: "Velveeta"
MacQueen's Quinterly; "Concerning Whisky," "Waking Alone After Drinking Too Much Wine in Umbria," and "Where are you, Walt Whitman?"
Ice On a Hot Stove: "Cheerleaders at Forty," "Cured," "Tool Box"
Pilgrimage: "After Ruysch's *Still-Life with Fruit and Insects*"
Poetry East: "Refugee"
Serving House Journal: "Cheerleaders at Forty," "Gender Studies: Why Men Fail at Small Talk," "Gestation"
South Carolina Review: "A Scatalogical Scat," "Tool Box"
Southeast Review: "Cured," winner of the Gearhart Poetry Prize
Still: The Journal: "An Explanation," winner of the Editor's Prize
Weekly Hubris: "Considering the Continued Use of Insects as Literary Metaphors," "What Remains," "What They Drank"
Writers by the River: "Concerning Whisky"

My gratitude to my colleagues on the Converse MFA faculty for their encouragement while I worked on these poems.

A special thanks in particular for the many years of friendship, support, and the occasional late-night whisky to Claire Bateman, Marlin Barton, Suzanne Cleary, Walter Cummins, Denise Duhamel, Gary Jackson, Lisa Hase-Jackson, Angela Kelly, Thomas E. Kennedy, Joseph Mayes, Robert Olmstead, Leslie Pietrzyk, and Richard Tillinghast.

And a sincere thanks to Albert Goldbarth for the good talks, the enduring friendship, the great poems, and for all the bacon.

Finally, my thanks to Susan and Hunter for the joy and for the music.

About the Author

Rick Mulkey is the author of six collections including *Ravenous: New & Selected Poems*, *Toward Any Darkness*, *Before the Age of Reason*, and *Bluefield Breakdown*. Individual poems and essays have appeared widely, including *Poetry East*, *Georgia Review*, *Crab Orchard Review*, *The Literary Review*, *Shenandoah*, *Poetry Daily*, and the anthologies *American Poetry: the Next Generation*, *The Southern Poetry Anthology: Volumes I and II*, and *A Millennial Sampler of South Carolina Poetry*, among others. His awards include the Hawthornden Fellowship, the Charles Angoff Award from *The Literary Review*, and the Gearhart Poetry Prize from *Southeast Review*. Mulkey is director and co-founder of the Converse Low Residency MFA.

Our Mission

BRICK ROAD

POETRY PRESS

The mission of Brick Road Poetry Press is to publish and promote poetry that entertains, amuses, edifies, and surprises a wide audience of appreciative readers. We are not qualified to judge who deserves to be published, so we concentrate on publishing what we enjoy. Our preference is for poetry geared toward dramatizing the human experience in language rich with sensory image and metaphor, recognizing that poetry can be, at one and the same time, both familiar as the perspiration of daily labor and as outrageous as a carnival sideshow.

Available from Brick Road Poetry Press

BRICK ROAD
POETRY PRESS
www.brickroadpoetrypress.com

The Word in Edgewise by Sean M. Conrey

Household Inventory by Connie Jordan Green

Practice by Richard M. Berlin

A Meal Like That by Albert Garcia

Cracker Sonnets by Amy Wright

Things Seen by Joseph Stanton

Battle Sleep by Shannon Tate Jonas

Lauren Bacall Shares a Limousine by Susan J. Erickson

Ambushing Water by Danielle Hanson

Having and Keeping by David Watts

Assisted Living by Erin Murphy

Credo by Steve McDonald

The Deer's Bandanna by David Oates

Creation Story by Steven Owen Shields

Touring the Shadow Factory by Gary Stein

American Mythology by Raphael Kosek

Waxing the Dents by Daniel Edward Moore

Also Available from Brick Road Poetry Press

BRICK ROAD
POETRY PRESS
www.brickroadpoetrypress.com

Dancing on the Rim by Clela Reed

Possible Crocodiles by Barry Marks

Pain Diary by Joseph D. Reich

Otherness by M. Ayodele Heath

Drunken Robins by David Oates

Damnatio Memoriae by Michael Meyerhofer

Lotus Buffet by Rupert Fike

The Melancholy MBA by Richard Donnelly

Two-Star General by Grey Held

Chosen by Toni Thomas

Etch and Blur by Jamie Thomas

Water-Rites by Ann E. Michael

Bad Behavior by Michael Steffen

Tracing the Lines by Susanna Lang

Rising to the Rim by Carol Tyx

Treading Water with God by Veronica Badowski

Rich Man's Son by Ron Self

Just Drive by Robert Cooperman

The Alp at the End of My Street by Gary Leising

About the Prize

BRICK ROAD

POETRY PRESS

The Brick Road Poetry Prize, established in 2010, is awarded annually for the best book-length poetry manuscript. Entries are accepted August 1st through November 1st. The winner receives $1000 and publication. For details on our preferences and the complete submission guidelines, please visit our website at www.brickroadpoetrypress.com.

Winners of the Brick Road Poetry Prize

2019

Return of the Naked Man by Robert Tremmel

2018

Speaking Parts by Beth Ruscio

2017

Touring the Shadow Factory by Gary Stein

2016

Assisted Living by Erin Murphy

2015

Lauren Bacall Shares a Limousine by Susan J. Erickson

2014

Battle Sleep by Shannon Tate Jonas

2013

Household Inventory by Connie Jordan Green

2012

The Alp at the End of My Street by Gary Leising

2011

Bad Behavior by Michael Steffen

2010

Damnatio Memoriae by Michael Meyerhofer

www.ingramcontent.com/pod-product-compliance
Lightning Source LLC
Chambersburg PA
CBHW022037090426
42741CB00007B/1097